Orland

Ten Motets

Edited by Clive Wearing

Oxford University Press
Music Department, 37 Dover Street, London W1X 4AH

Preface

The career of Orlandus Lassus (1532-94) reflects the cosmopolitan world of sixteenth-century Europe, when, even though travel was extremely arduous, national boundaries had little significance for artists and musicians. Thus, he was born in Mons (Belgium), but at about the age of 12, he entered the service of the Viceroy of Sicily (Ferrante Gonzaga), and spent his formative years in Palermo, Naples, and Milan. In about 1553 he was appointed *maestro di capella* at St John Lateran in Rome, but after a few months he returned to the Netherlands on hearing the news of his parents' fatal illness. His first published works appeared in 1555, and it is just possible that he visited England at about this time. He accepted an invitation to join the *capella* of Duke Albrecht of Bavaria at Munich in 1557, where he remained for the rest of his life, though continuing to travel extensively. There is a considerable amount of biographical material which has survived, including 57 letters dating from 1572-91, the majority of which are addressed to his employer in familiar terms, wandering from language to language with evident delight. It is clear that, at least in his earlier years, he was an engaging companion - witty, urbane, earthy, and highly intelligent.

Perhaps the most important single document regarding the conditions at the Munich Court is the account of the wedding of Duke Wilhelm (Albrecht's son) to Renée of Lorraine in February 1568. The author, Massimo Troiano, was employed as an 'alto' in the *capella* and, in the years 1567-70, was becoming known as a composer of *villanelle*. The wedding account (2 editions entitled *Discorsi*, Munich, 1568; and *Dialoghi*, Venice, 1569) contains a chapter which deals with the organization and personnel of the *capella*. From this chapter we learn that the singers performed Mass every morning in the Court Chapel, and that they were joined by the wind instruments on Sundays and Feast Days, and for Vespers on Saturdays and the Vigils of Major Feasts.

Lassus's sacred music forms the most important portion of his output, though he wrote works in every genre current at the time. His sacred works include some 65 masses, 550 'motets', 102 magnificats, 32 hymns, and many other liturgical pieces. To select ten motets from such an output is a very difficult task, though it is possible to reduce the total of 550 by omitting the Psalm settings, Marian Antiphons, hymns, sequences, and canticles from this category. Mus MS 2744 at the Bayerische Staatsbibliothek, Munich, contains 40 Offertories for Advent and Lent, in the correct liturgical order, which were published in 1585 (in a different order). This manuscript provides us with an accurate method of determining the liturgical function of Nos. 4, 5, and 9. I have assigned the remainder to specific feasts by an examination of the texts, with reference to contemporary liturgical sources.

The year 1580 was of great importance in the liturgical history of the Munich Court for, following the death of Duke Albrecht in 1579, the reforms of the Council of Trent were then adopted. Works published before that date were intended for use in the special liturgy of the Diocese of Freising (in which Munich lay). Unfortunately, we cannot state with certainty that those published after 1580 were intended for the new liturgy, since it is possible that they were written at an earlier date. However, Mus MS 2744 carries dates between 1581 and 1583, and *Veni sancte spiritus* in Mus MS 15 is dated 1577. We must also remember that these manuscripts are not in Lassus's own hand, and that the dates refer to the work of a copyist.

Among other things, the Council of Trent decreed that instruments were excluded from church music in Advent and Lent, and are therefore inappropriate in Nos. 1, 4, 5, and 9; on the other hand, the title pages of the volumes containing Nos. 2, 3, 4, 6, 7, and 9 bear the rubric: 'suitable for voices and all kinds of instruments'. This conflicting evidence for Nos. 4 and 9 should certainly be resolved by excluding instruments.

Troiano, in his *Dialoghi*, is full of praise for the Munich *capella*, and for Lassus's direction of it: 'His [Lassus's] great skill, together with all the consistency and ingenuity of his art, enabled him to lead the singing by setting a tempo so exact and well judged, that just as the sound of the trumpet inspires warriors to take courage, so the expert singers took strength and vigour from his direction, to let their voices flow with liveliness, sweetness, and sonority.' Intonation and blend also concerned Troiano: '. . . throughout a Mass that Orlando had given them, they did not deviate more than three commas above or below the note. And another thing, which is both marvellous and satisfactory for the listener, the sound from these controlled voices was so well integrated that the best ears could not distinguish one from another.'

In this collection, I have transcribed all works from the first known published editions, but they were all also included in the *Magnum Opus Musicum* (1604), a vast compilation of 'motets' published posthumously by Lassus's sons, which has formed the basis of the Breitkopf & Härtel *Sämtliche Werke* (1894–). I have transposed Nos. 4, 5, and 9 in order to avoid extremely low notes for the Alto lines. A case exists, of course, for downward transposition of a fourth in Nos. 3, 6, and 8, which have the high *chiavette* clefs but, in the absence of firm evidence linking this practice to Munich, I have left these works at their original pitch.

With the exception of Nos. 2 and 7, all these motets are freely composed. No. 2, *Resonet in laudibus*, is a *cantus firmus* composition with the melody in the Tenor, in the first and third parts. The melody (better known in its German form, *Joseph lieber, Joseph mein*) appears in a fifteenth-century manuscript at Leipzig University, where it accompanied a scene in a nativity play. Lassus slightly alters the rhythm from time to time, and casts the work in a kind of 'Responsory' form (ABCDB). Further versions of this melody are known by Johann Walter, Jacob Regnart, Jacob Handl, Michael Praetorius, and even Brahms and Reger. No. 7, *Veni sancte spiritus*, is also a *cantus firmus* composition using a plainsong Antiphon. The same *cantus firmus* appears in Mus MS 52 at the Bayerische Staatsbibliothek, in an anonymous 5-part composition described as the Psalm Antiphon for first Vespers of Pentecost, an ascription confirmed in the Freising Diocese liturgical books.

No. 8, *Tibi laus*, is in two parts whose texts appear to bear little relation to each other. The *Prima Pars* text was also provided with a 4-voice version by Lassus which ends at the words 'O beata Trinitas'; but it is clear that this 5-voice setting cannot finish at the same point. Three possible explanations come to mind: either these texts have been deliberately juxtaposed, perhaps by Lassus himself; this juxtaposition is to be found in some liturgical source; or perhaps Lassus joined two separate works together, replacing an original *Secunda Pars*, which he considered unsatisfactory. Perhaps the explanation is to be found in Sherlock Holmes's so far unpublished monograph on *The Polyphonic Motets of Orlando di Lasso*!

The four 4-part works (Nos. 1, 4, 5, and 9) are stylistically similar with close, almost canonic, imitation of striking melodic material at the start of each section of the text. Nos. 3, 6, and 8 show Lassus at his most exuberant, in settings which abound in felicitous madrigalian touches and restrained chromatic colouring. No. 10, *Timor et tremor*, however, is one of Lassus's most famous essays in chromaticism, here put to the service of a powerful text which, in turn, stimulated the composer to produce one of his most moving and dramatic settings.

CLIVE WEARING
London May 1981

1. CONFORTAMINI ET IAM

Déus nós-ter re - trĭ - bu - et iu - dĭ - ci -

Déus nós-ter re - trĭ - bu - et iu - dĭ -

- us nós - ter re - trĭ - bu - et iu - dĭ - ci -

Dé - us nós - ter re - trĭ - bu - et iu -

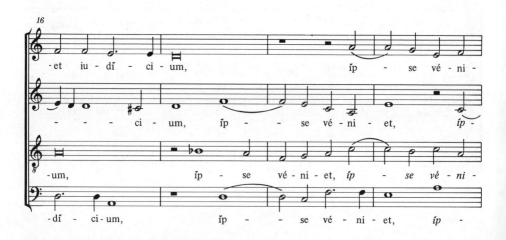

- et iu - dĭ - ci - um, ĭp - se vé - ni -

- - ci - um, ĭp - - se vé - ni - et, ĭp -

- um, ĭp - se vé - ni - et, ĭp - se vé - ni -

- dĭ - ci - um, ĭp - - se vé - ni - et, ĭp -

- et, ĭp - se vé - ni - et, ĭp - se vé - ni - et,

- se vé - ni - et, ĭp - se vé - ni -

- et, ĭp - se vé - ni - et, ĭp - se vé - ni - et,

- se vé - ni - et, ĭp - se vé - ni - et, ut

2. RESONET IN LAUDIBUS

6

*Note values halved
Original time signature: **◐3** (except Altus: **₵3**)

TRIA *[SECUNDA PARS]
49 [SOLI]

*In Bass only
**Original time signature: 𝄵

Ís - ra - el, ap - pá - ru - it in Ís - ra - el, ap - pá - ru-

-it in Ís - ra - el, ap - pá - ru - it in Ís - ra - el, ap - pá - ru-

ap - pá - ru - it, *ap - pá - ru - it* in Ís - ra - el, ap -

-it, ap - pá - ru - it in Ís - ra - el per ___ Ma - rĭ - am vĭr - gi - nem est

-it, ap - pá - ru - it in Ís - ra - el _____ per Ma - rĭ - am

- pá - ru - it ___ in Ís - ra - el per Ma - rĭ - am vĭr - gi - nem,

ná - - - - - tus rex, per ___ Ma - rĭ - am

vĭr - gi - nem est ná - tus rex, *per Ma - rí - am vír -*

per Ma - rĭ - am vĭr - gi - nem est

vĭr - gi - nem, *per Ma - rí - am vír - - gi - nem,*

- gi - nem est _____ ná - tus rex, per

ná - tus rex, *per Ma - rí - am vír - gi - nem*

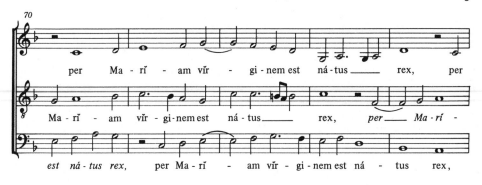

per Ma - rí - am vǐr - gi - nem est ná - tus _____ rex, per

Ma - rí - am vǐr - gi - nem est ná - tus _____ rex, per _____ Ma - rí -

est ná - tus rex, per Ma - rí - am vǐr - gi - nem est ná - tus rex,

Ma - rí - am vǐr - gi - nem est ná - tus rex, est _____ ná - tus rex.

- am vír - gi - nem est ná - tus rex. _____

per Ma - rí - am vír - gi - nem _____ est ná - tus rex.

TERTIA PARS [TUTTI]

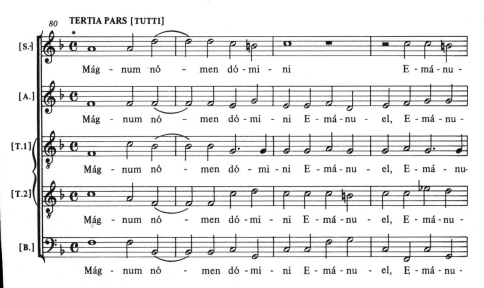

[S.] Mág - num nó - men dó - mi - ni E - má - nu -

[A.] Mág - num nó - men dó - mi - ni E - má - nu - el, E - má - nu -

[T.1] Mág - num nó - men dó - mi - ni E - má - nu - el, E - má - nu -

[T.2] Mág - num nó - men dó - mi - ni E - má - nu - el, E - má - nu -

[B.] Mág - num nó - men dó - mi - ni E - má - nu - el, E - má - nu -

*Original time signature: ₵

10

*Note values halved

Original time signature: 𝄵3

3. VIDENTES STELLAM MAGI

4. LEVABO OCULOS

*original: *ut*

5. DOMINE FAC MECUM

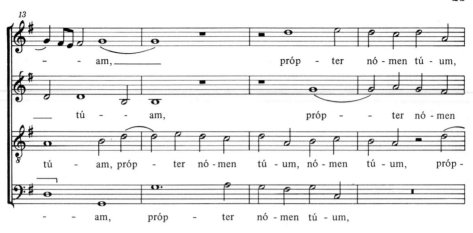

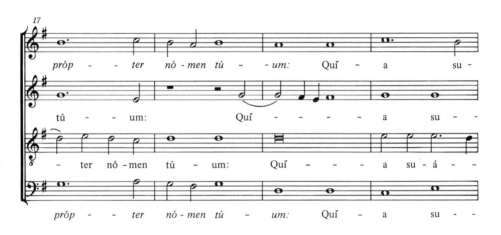

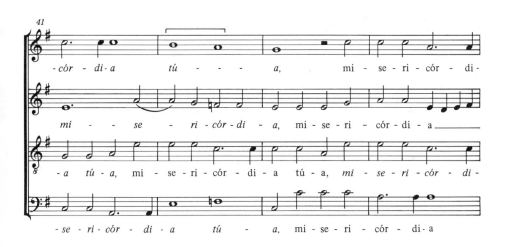

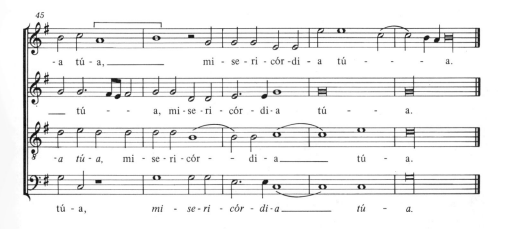

6. CHRISTUS RESURGENS

7. VENI SANCTE SPIRITUS

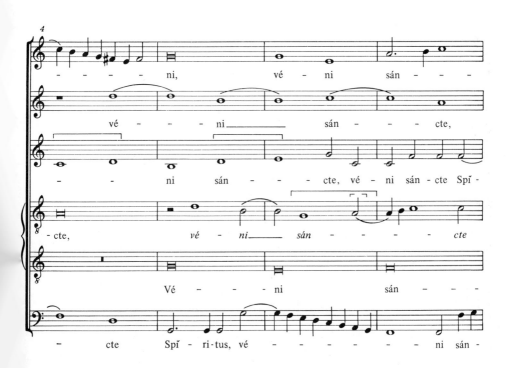

34

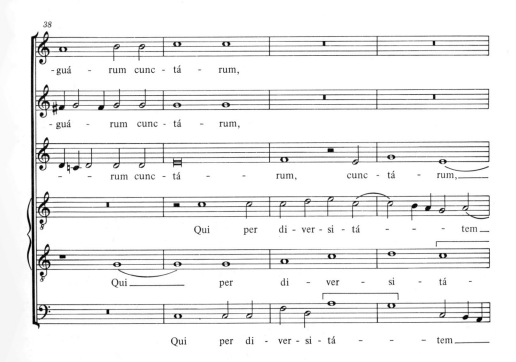

38

40

8. TIBI LAUS, TIBI GLORIA

42

*Note values halved

9. EXALTABO TE

51

10. TIMOR ET TREMOR

*tie editorial
**original: *miserere mei*

54

*If the low D is impossible, sing either a high D, or a minim A.

56

42 **SECUNDA PARS**

58

*original: *quoniam*

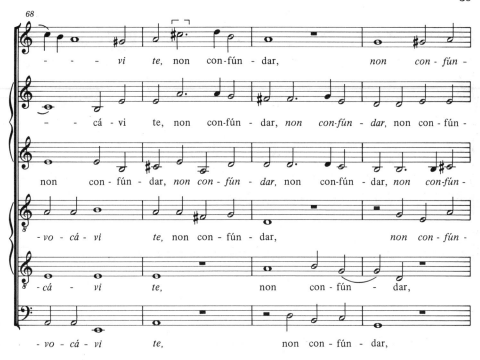

*original: *in aeternum*

Reproduced and printed by Halstan & Co. Ltd., Amersham, Bucks., England